At the Market

Written by Monica Hughes

Illustrated by Lisa Williams

Ed and Auntie Nina buy sunglasses.

£5
£5

Ed and Auntie Nina buy sunhats.

£8
£5
£10

Ed and Auntie Nina buy flip-flops.

£40
£4
£10
£7
£7
£8
£9

Ed and Auntie Nina buy books.

HOT
HOT
HOT
£5
BEACH DAYS
£2·50
BUY 1
GET 1
FREE

Ed and Auntie Nina

buy fruit juice.

£3
£2

Ed and Auntie Nina
buy fruit.

£2.50
£1.50

Ed and Auntie Nina buy...

WILD ANIMALS

...a big bag.